T0161260

SKY
WRI
TEI
NGS

NASSER HUSSAIN

MAPS BY
MATTHEW STEPHENSON

COACH HOUSE BOOKS | YYZ

first edition

Published with the generous assistance of the Canada Council for the Arts and the Ontario Arts Council. Coach House Books also acknowledges the support of the Government of Canada through the Canada Book Fund.

LIBRARY AND ARCHIVES CANADA CATALOGUING IN PUBLICATION

Hussain, Nasser 1972-, author
    SKY WRI TEI NGS / Nasser Hussain.

Poems.
Issued in print and electronic formats.
ISBN 978-1-55245-371-1 (softcover)

        I. Title.

PR6108.U77S59 2018   C821'.92   C2018-903926-4
                                                      C2018-903927-2

SKY WRI TEI NGS is available as an ebook: ISBN 978 1 77056 563 0 (EPUB), ISBN 978 1 77056 564 7 (PDF)

Purchase of the print version of this book entitles you to a free digital copy. To claim your ebook of this title, please email sales@chbooks.com with proof of purchase. (Coach House Books reserves the right to terminate the free digital download offer at any time.)

DED ICA TED TOO:

LPK MCK
KAK KJK KIP JAC
BEN JEE
GEO FRY KRA MER
OLK
LRB EAR

WEL CUM ABO ARD

KNO SMO KIN
BUC KLE UPP

KIT TEN HOK

THO THE SUB JCT TOF

AER IAL

NAV IGA SHN

ISE

JIN ERR ALL AEI

CON SID ERD

NEW

ITH ATH

OCK YOO PID

THE MIN DZO MEN

MOR EOR LES

FRO THE

STA RTS

AIR TRA VEL

MIG RAT ION

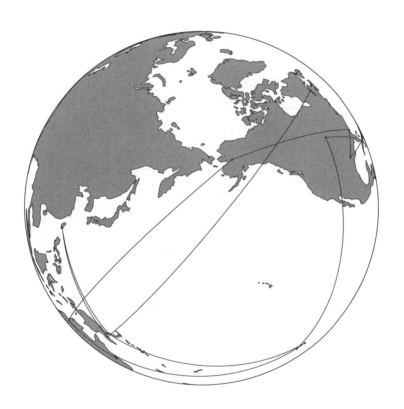

ALF AAH BET

AAA BBB CCC

GGG HHH
      KKK LLL
MMM
PPP   RRR
SSS TTT UUU

YYY

DEC ODE

COD ECO DEC
ODE COD ECO
DEC ODE COD

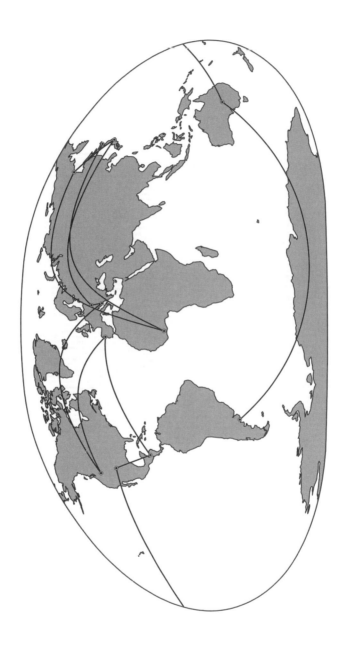

OHH OHH

```
OBO  OGO  OHO
OKO  OLO  OMO
ONO  OPO  ORO
OTO  OXO  OYO
```

STO RIS

THE ASP BIT
CLE OPA TRA

ABE MAY AXE
ISA ACS ARM
BUT JAH LET ABE OFF

ANU CAN FLY
AND AUK CAN FLY
EVE CAN NOT

EVE ATE THE APP LES
AND SAW THE LIE

DAV GOT COM PUT ERS
BUT HAL CAN NOT SAY YES

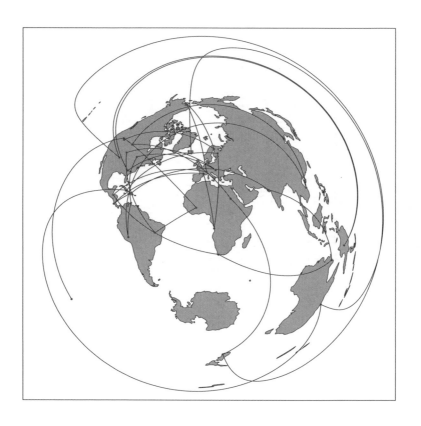

APE MAN

BOB BOI BOY
BRA BUB BUD
CAD CUB CUR
CUZ DAD DIK
DOG DUD FAG
FOP GUV GUY
HIS HOG JOE
LAD MEN NOB
POP RAJ RAM
ROD SAP SIR
SOL SOT SUN

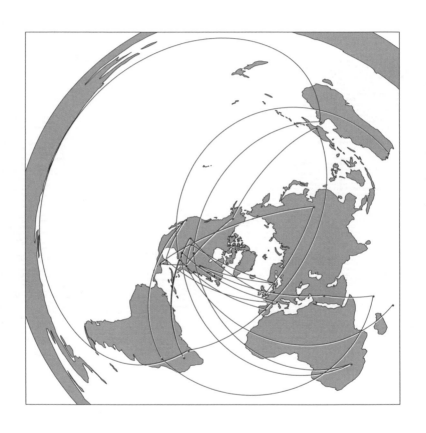

HST ORY

ALL AGO, ELL CID MET THE MEN.
MID LAX LIP, SEZ:
'HAS YOO GOT GUT?'
'GOT EAR, AND SAP DAT BZZ?'
'DEN IRE, MOB, GET MAD, HIT BIG, AND RUN.'

BOX DRE AMS

ALI BOO KLU
        KLX
        KLN
        KKK

ALI GOT MAD
ALI GOT BAD, MAN

ALI FLO
ALI TOO
AND ALI FRO

ALI BOX FOE
BAM HIS EAR
BUS DAT LIP
DIP AND DAP
SLY MID MAT
TIP TOP PRO

ALI HAD HIM
        DOA

REF
SAY ONE
SAY SIX
SAY TEN

SAY TKO

FLY HIE (FOR BEE)

IZT BRD?

PLN?

KNO!

SPR MAN!

(LEX LUT HOR: RUN!)

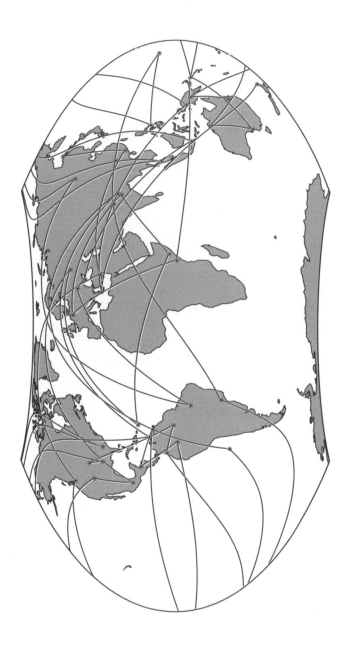

EAT (FOR MIC LEE)

OHH CAN ADA
EAT TIM BIT
    KIT KAT
    POO TEN
    TIC TAC

TEX MEX PEZ
BBQ BIB

PAT GUT
     (GAS)

NUT MIX
TEA CUP
RAW PEA
DRY BUN
PIG EAR

HOT PAN AND
COQ AUX VIN

SIP SUP
BON BON
RUM SOT
    (HIC)

NOM NOM
MMM MMM

SLI GHT DEL AYS

TEN DRR BUT TON (FOR GER TIE)

ROA STA COW; MUT TON; BRE AKF AST; SUG ARR;
CRA NBE RRI ESS; MLK; EGS; APP LES; TAI ELS;
LUN CHH; CUP; RUE BRB; SIN GLE; PHI SSH; CAK;
CUS TRD; POT ATO; ASP ARA GUS; BUT TER; END
OFF SUM MER; SAU SAG ESS; SEL URY; VEE LUH;
VEG TBL; COO KIN; CHI KEN; PAS TRY; CRE EAM;
CUC UMM BER; DIN NER; DIN DIN; EAT; SAL ADD;
SAU CES; SAL MON; ORA NGE; COK COA; AND CLE
ARS SOU PAN DOR ANG ESS AND OTM EAL; SAL ADD
DRE SSI NGS AND ANA RTI CHO KUH; ASS ENT ERR
INN AHH TAB BUL.

SHE FLY

HER HAJ WAS TUF.
HER CHI WAS LOW.

SHE WAS WAY FAR OFF.
DUE TOO GPS MAP ERR ORS

SHE SMS HER BUD FOR AID:

'SAY, CAN YOO SEE
MAR ALA GOO?'

DEL ADE
FOR HRS

OLD MAG AZI INE
OLD BOO KMA RKS
OLD TEA WOE

. . .

ATL AST
TAK OFF!

CUT FOR JED DAH VIA BOM BAY

LON GHA ULS
SEA TTI LTS
CUT LEG ROO MOF

BUC KLE UPP —
COM INN INN FOR THE LAN DIN!

AHH,
KAA BAA.

OMG.

FIT BIT

TRY HUG
TRY JOG
TRY BEG

ASK FOR PEN
GET ARM

HEW SAW CUT

IRK INK
RUE AGE

ZIG ZAG

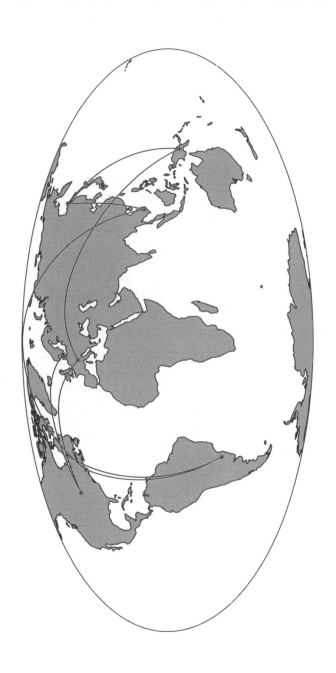

SOU NDS

```
AGH AHH ACH
AIE OHH HOO
AYE ERM YAH
```

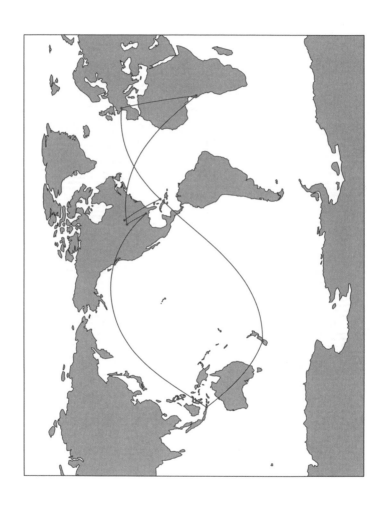

APP REY ZZV OUS

PST MON AMI
TOU EST FOU

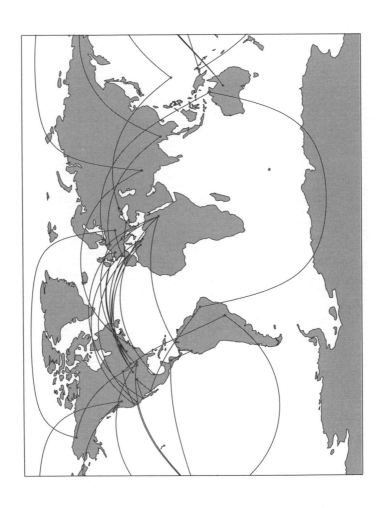

BOD IES

BRO,
ABS AGE.

JAB THE GYM GUY –
SEE? ABS AIL.

LAT JUT. NUT LIP. ILL SAC.

TIP TOP TOE FAT.
HIP HOP GUM JAM.

BMI BOD
BUF GUT
TAT SAG
MAW POX

HEH:

HES URN FIT.

AYE AYE

THY WRY SHY GUY
TRY SPY PLY

VIE AND DIE
LIE AND BUY

AND

CRY AND CRY
AND CRY AND
CRY

OHH HAI:

TRY MYE
SKY PIE

EVA AND BOB

EVA AND BOB
(HER MAD COW BOY TOY)
ATE ALL THE PIE.
CUT AND RUN, KID.
THE LAD LAY LOW
BUT HIS MRS
MRS HIM.

DES IRE

NOT MRS MUM NOR MAM
TSK TSK VIR JIN SIN

AMI AMO

FAB BED
FOR GAY
MEN
AND LEZ
COY TUS

WOW, RUG!

SAY AAH OHH OHH

BUN FUN
PAT BUM
TUG NUT
PAD BRA

SUB DOM

TUT TUT ROD
HER BIG BOI

AMO LUV ART

ERR UMM SHY ACT

DOM EMO HEE HEE

HUG

IMA TAP DAT

INT ERR NOT

THE SEL FIE
    STI CKS
THE MAT RIX
    GLI TCH
THE SNP CHT
    SNP BCK

ALL THE
FAC EBO OOK
DAT AHH

    TEN THU MBS UPP
AND EMO GEE SHE EPS

SAY:
YAS SSS SSS!

DOU BLE CLI CKS HIT.

POE TRY ISS NUS THA TST AYS NEW

PET ALS ONA WET BLA ACK BOW

ORD ERS

ABC DEF
MNO RST

PAL IND ROM ESS (FOR AET HER INN)

AIR ANA RIA
AMO RER OMA

ROT AVA TOR
RED IVI DER
MAT AMA TAM
CIN EGE NIC
MAL AYA LAM

REN OLO NER
STE PON NOP ETS

ABU TTT UBA
HAH HAH HAH

AMA NAP AIN AMA NIA PAN AMA
AMA NAP LAN ACA NAL PAN AMA

CHI KEN ORP AST AHH?

SOR REE FOR ANY
INK UNN VIN YEN SUH

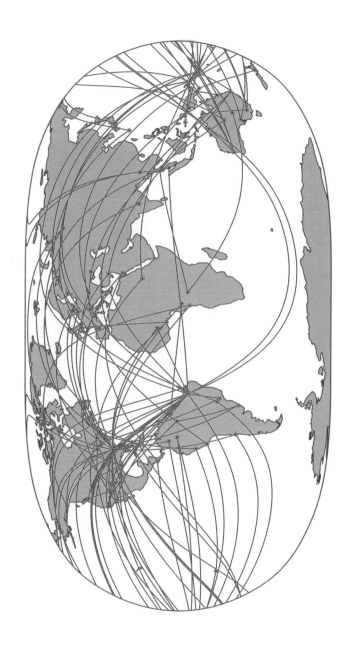

THE ARK

GET DOS AHI
    DOS KOI
    DOS EEL
    DOS COW AND CUB
        BEE AND BOA
        YAK AND LEO
        DOE AND DOG
    DOS APE ANT ASP AUK
    DOS BAT RAT CAT CUR AND MOG

EWE AND GNU
GAD FLY AND MAY FLY
RAM NAG AND PET PIG
FAT HOG PUG AND PUP
THE LAM KID AND THE FOX KIT
THE ELK ROC AND YAK
THE SEA SOW AND TAU RUS

(ARF BAA BAY BZZ COO GRR
KAW MEW MOO YIP WAG PAW)

AND GET

ONE NOA
AND HIS EMS ARA

ONE HAM
AND NEL ATA MUK

ONE SHM
AND HIS BAE

ONE JAP ETH
AND ADA TAN ESE

ALL THE DNA AND RNA

GET THE HAY
FOR THE POO PIT
GET THE AFT WET
DRY THE BOW OAR
ROW THE PEN

YAY! SEE THE TOR?
                    ARA RAT.

YEP YOO CAN

ACT DIM
DRY FRY VEG

LET BET LIE
HOP MAP LAP
MOP PET PEE

KID MAY ROB
SUE RAP MIX

BOW ROW

LOL MOO

BAG BAT
SAG SAT
TAG TOE
NAG TAX
SAP SAP

CAP SIN
SKI RUN

DRY GAB
VEX YAK

GAG RIG

THE SKY (ONE)

THE SKY WAS THE SKY

THE SKY WAS HER
SHE WAS THE SKY

THE SKY WAS SLY
THE SKY WAS INK

THE SKY WAS SOH IGH

THE SKY WAS
THE SKY ALL DAY

THE SKY (TOO)

HIT THE SKY,
AND THE SKY HID.

THE SKY WAS SLY.
    THE SKY FEL.

HER MOM
WAS EVE,

HER DAD WAS
THE DAY

WHO LIT
HIS RIB.

THE DAM
DOG DAY END.

NOW,
NEW
EVE.

SAY SHH,
SEE SKY.

THE SKY (TRI)

EVE SET THE SUN

FOR HER

HER KIN
HER FAV
HER ALL

HER PET ION
HER RED SKY

(GOO DNI GHT)

THE CAT   THE HAT

The sun did not was too wet sat the All wet
day

sat sat And 'How had' Too wet out And too sat
the did all.

all was Sit! Sit! Sit! Sit! and did not not
one bit.

How

saw him the mat! And saw him! The Cat   the
Hat! and 'Why you sit?'

'wet the sun But can fun!'

the cat new   the Cat   the Hat 'lot you not
all' did not and was out the for the day.

but our   'cat Cat   the Hat you not not
not not out!'

'Now! Now!' the cat. 'not bad,' the Cat   the
Hat. 'can fun you.'

'Put!' the. 'fun all! Put!' the 'not!'

'!' the cat. 'not let one! cup hat! But not
all can!' the cat.

'now!' the cat. 'cup and the top hat! can can
the and toy and and can hop and the! but not
all! not all!

'now! fun fun but can the cup and the and the
can the can the toy and toy man! And can red!
can the hop the not all. Not all...'

the cat his the and and saw all the!

and our, too. pot! not. not our lit. 'not not
one!'

'now you!' the the cat. 'Now! You toy, the
you are and you our new you not our not you
get out!' the the pot.

'but lot!' the Cat   the Hat. The the pot.
'not not! And,' the Cat   the Hat, '!'

And ran out and the Cat   the Hat box. big
red box. was 'now,' the cat.

got top tip hat 'fun-box' the cat. 'box now.'
the cat bow.

'the. See new. And one and. not you. fun. out
the box. and One! And ran. 'how One and?'
And and not had One and our 'not!'

'not not! out out!' the the pot.

the Cat   the Hat 'are.' and pat 'are fun
wet, wet, wet day.'

the cat 'fly,' the Cat   the Hat

'not the!' the the pot. 'not fly. not. the the
hit! not not one bit!'

and saw run the saw the the the

and One ran ran! the saw new! her the are and
red saw one the her bed!

ran big and. and and big and all bad and 'Not
the way! she say!'

our and our 'her way she say? she not way!'

the 'saw her. can get rid One!'

And 'can get bet. bet can get yet!'

let. and had. had. the cat, 'say. and!'

the cat 'not our…'

the the box the cat sad

the 'has. Yes. But she big and big and can
not way all!'

And! Who was the? the cat! the Cat   the Hat.
all and.

saw him all the the and the, and the, and
the, and the, and the, and the, and the and
the cup, and the, and the. And put was tip
hat.

our and she 'Did any fun? did? And and did
not say. her the? her?

DEP END - ONE (FOR BCW)

RED

    THE

DEP END – TOO (FOR SUS)

SUM OCH DEP END
SUP ONA

RED WEL ELB
ARR OGG

LAZ EDW ITH RAI
NWA TER

BES IDE THE WIT
CHI KEN.

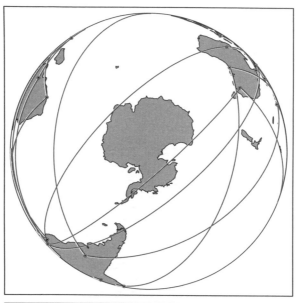

EUN OIA (FOR BOK)

ENF ETR ERD THE SEN TEN
SEZ REP RES FRE ESP ECH.
THE TEX DEL ETE SSE LEC
TED LET TER SWE SEE THE
REE VEE ERD EGS EGE ETE
REG EKT MET ERD VER SEH:
THE SEZ TET, THE TER CET
EVE NLE SSC ENE SEL EVE
ESE NGR EKE. HEE REB ELS.
HES ETS NEW PRE CED ENT SSS.

FOR WAL TER WHT MAN

MEE MEE MEE

MEE MEE
MEE MEE

                (BAR BAR ICK YOP!)

MEE MEE MEE

MEE MEE
MEE MEE

BUS BOY

HIM CUS
ALL
WOR KIN
DAY

ALL
CLA TER
AND
DRI NKS
AND
SHO UTS
AND
NOI SEZ
TIL
THE
WOR KIN
DAY

END

LUV

PHI LOS

THE SEX WAS
HEA VEN

LIP KIS LIP
    KIS EAR
    KIS EYE
    KIS HIM
    KIS HER
    KIS BUM
    KIS ALL

YES YES YES

JAC AND THE

FIE FLY
FOE FUM

GAM ERG ATE

ALT RIG HTS
AND DEL ETE

THE BRO ODE: DOX HER   TAR HER   FUK HER
                  COW HER   SUE HER
                  POP HER

                  GET HER

KEY KEY KEY
CRY CRY CRY

THE NET MOB ALL
ILL ILK GET NUT

LOL LOL
ALL DAY

KEY KEY KEY
YAK YAK YAK

YOO CAN YOO TUB YER WAY, PAY PAL,
BUT SAY WOW:

- SHE BAD ASS

GOS SIP/ TWO CAT

— OHH HAI!

    — OHH HAI!

— BLA BLA BLA

    — YEP YEP YAH

— YOO KNO PAT?

    — SHE BAD!

— DAN WAS HER MAN

    — BUT SHE GOT WIT PAM!

— YAH, SUB URB MOM

    — YEP, HER GUT WAS BIG

— YAH, BUT HER PIE WAS HOT

    — TUT TUT. STI HOE!

— BUT DAT CAR!

    — DAT CAR...

— YAH, SHE WAS HOT, YET NOT.

    — YAH, SHE WAS HET BUT SET!

— AHH. AHA. SAY WAT?

    — SHE BLO HIS JON SON?

— NAH, SHE PAW HER RUG

    — OOH, WOW – SHE BAD!

— ASK HER!

                      — PAT: NOT THY BIZ.

                            BZZ OFF.

ISL AMO PHO BIA

USA USA USA USA USA USA USA
USA USA USA USA USA USA USA
USA TOO WIT TER HAT ERS USA
MAK EAM ERI CAG REA TAG AIN
USA USA USA USA USA USA USA
USA USA USA USA USA USA USA

TMI

THE COP AND THE CON
AND THE CIA KNO ALL

PAN HOP TIC ONS LOG
OUR SMS, OUR SLY SEX,
OUR NAU GHT INE SSS, ETC.

GOT THE DEC ODE ERR.
GOT THE GAG ORD ERS.
GOT THE TOR TUR ERS.

HEY!
LIT TLE SPY
WHO LES
PEE PER:

GET OUT!

PAY DAY

SHE LOW.
GOT HOT GIG
BUT NOT MOE PAY
BIG WAD? NAW.

GOT TNA AND MBA
GOT TIP JAR TRI CKS
AND CAN EKE OUT ONE DOL LAR PER DAY

ANY WAY
SHE CAN

NOT FUN VAC ATI ONS FOR HER
FAR FAR OFF (SHE GOT KIN IN PAT TER SON, BUT...)

AND THO THE ADS
SAY 'BUY'
SHE GOT MAX NOT.

THE ROT TEN BOS
REP ITI TIV ELY
SQU EZE AND SQU EZE AND SQU EZE HER SUM ORE

TIL HER BOD POP.

ELL TEE DEE

UCK UNE UNG
UNE   USK
UNG USK
     USH UDE
USH UDE UCK
UDE UNG

TIM NGS

MON TUE WED THR FRI SAT SUN

JAN FEB MAR APR MAY JUN JUL AUG SEP   NOV DEC

HRS DAY
MOS YRS

ERE AND ERA

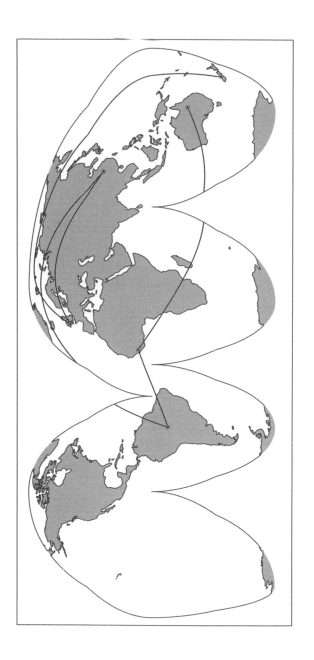

JER NAL ISM

WHO
WOT
WUH AIR
WYE
WIN

ALF AAH BET (2)

AIE BEE SEE
DEE EAT EPH
GEE ACH EYE
JFK ELM ENS
OHH PEE CUE
ERR ESS TEA
YOO VEE
DUB BLE YOO
SEX WYE ZIA

(EYE CAN SAY THE ABC EZE)

THE KEY

EIN STE INS

FRM ULA SEZ

ENE RGI

ISM ASS.

SEE?

    — YER LIG HTS.

LAU GHT ERR

HEE HEE
HAH HAH
HEE HAW
GUF HAW
    EEK!
  (PEE PEE)

HEH HEH HEH

HOO...

THA NKS FOR
TRA VEL LIN
 WIT HUS.

THE LOC ALL
TIM EIS SIX
 PEE EMM.

HOP YOO HAD
APL ESS ENT
 FLI GHT.

   CYA.
 GOO DBY.

THE END

TRA VEL NOT ESS

TRA VEL NOT ESS

END NOT ESS

'KIT TEN HOK' is a transposition of the first
sentence of Wilbur and Orville Wright's book
The Early History of the Airplane (source:
Project Gutenberg)

'TEN DRR BUT TON (FOR GER TIE)' rewrites the
'Contents' page from the Food section of
Gertrude Stein's *Tender Buttons* (1997 Dover
edition, p. 20)

'DEP END – BCW' stands for Bill Carlos
Williams. (WCW, sadly, is not an airport.)

'THE CAT   THE HAT' is an erasure of the
original book that preserves only the punctu-
ation and the airports.

Airport codes were checked against the IATA
database, via their webpage:
www.iata.org/publications/Pages/code-
search.aspx

A world map with all airport codes can be
found at www.chbooks.com/SKYWRITEINGSmap.

Readers may also find Karl L. Swartz's website
(Great Circle Mapper) of interest:
www.gcmap.com

THA NKS:

ALL NAS' LBU COL LEA GUE SSS (ESP THE ZER OHS
  AND WIL SPR LNG)
SHO LBR OOK (FOR EDI TNG)
COA CHH OUS EBO OKS (ALA NNA, CRY STL, RAT
TRA YYY, ETC)
AND
DER ICK BOW LEE YOO

ACK KNO LED GEM ENT

'THE ARK' appeared in *Wretched Strangers*,
eds. Welsch and Lehoczky, Norwich: Boiler-
house Press 2018

The suggestion for 'THE CAT THE HAT' was Rob
Catto's. He lives in Leeds, and we had a beer
together once at the train station.

Nasser Hussain is a Lecturer in Literature and Creative Writing at Leeds Beckett University in the U.K. His first book, *boldface* was published in 2014. He holds a PhD in English from the University of York (U.K.), an MA in Creative Writing from the University of Windsor, and a BA in English from Queen's University.

Typeset in Andale Mono and Albertan Pro

Printed at the Coach House on bpNichol Lane in Toronto, Ontario, on Zephyr Antique Laid paper, which was manufactured, acid-free, in Saint-Jérôme, Quebec, from second-growth forests. This book was printed with vegetable-based ink on a 1973 Heidelberg KORD offset litho press. Its pages were folded on a Baumfolder, gathered by hand, bound on a Sulby Auto-Minabinda and trimmed on a Polar single-knife cutter.

Edited for the press by Susan Holbrook
Designed by Ricky Lima and Alana Wilcox
Cover design by Crystal Sikma
Cover art by Kevin Reinhardt
Author photo by Leeds Beckett University

Coach House Books
80 bpNichol Lane
Toronto ON M5S 3J4
Canada

416 979 2217
800 367 6360

mail@chbooks.com
www.chbooks.com